my
CHRISTIAN
FAITH

About this book

The titles in the *My Faith* collection are designed to introduce young children to the six world faiths and each focuses on a child and his or her family from a particular faith community. Whilst the approach and the language level are appropriate for young readers, some of the key concepts will need to be supported by sensitive clarification by an adult. The *Notes for Teachers and Parents* on pages 4 and 5 provide extra information to help develop children's knowledge and understanding of the different beliefs and traditions.

VISIT OUR WEBSITE www.evansbooks.co.uk

First published in this edition in 2006 by
Evans Brothers Limited
2A Portman Mansions
Chiltern St
London W1U 6NR

Printed in China by WKT Company Limited

British Library Cataloguing in Publication Data

Seaman, Alison
    My Christian faith. - (My Faith)
    1. Christianity - Juvenile literature   2. Christians - Juvenile literature
    I. Title
    230
    ISBN 023753226 3
    13 digit ISBN (from 1 January 2007) 9780237 53226 0

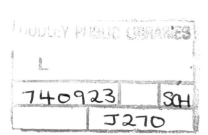
Editor: Su Swallow
Design: D.R. ink
Production: Jenny Mulvanny
Reading consultant: Lesley Clark, Reading and Language Information Centre
Series consultant: Alison Seaman, The National Society's Religious Education Centre
Commissioned photography: Gareth Boden

Acknowledgements

The authors and publishers would like to thank Daniel Alldis and his family. The authors would also like to thank the members of Holy Trinity, Eltham, for their help and cooperation in the preparation of this book.

For permission to reproduce copyright material the author and publishers gratefully acknowledge the following:

page 17 The Bridgeman Art Library; page 19 David Rose; page 25 Trevor Wood, Robert Harding; page 28 Kodak Ltd, Robert Harding; page 29 David Rose

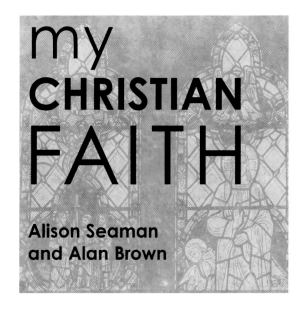

my CHRISTIAN FAITH

**Alison Seaman
and Alan Brown**

Evans

Contents

Notes for Teachers and Parents

Pages 6/7 A Christian is a follower of Jesus Christ. Jesus lived around two thousand years ago in the country we now call Israel. The word 'Christ' is from the Greek word which means 'anointed' and was the name given to Jesus by his followers. Sunday is the day Christians normally worship together because it is the day on which they believe Jesus rose from the dead. Churches vary in the types of worship they offer. Families will often worship together and many churches organise Sunday Schools in which children can participate.

Pages 8/9 The word 'church' can mean the building, (some Christian groups call the building by other names, e.g. chapel, citadel, meeting house) but it really means the people who belong to the church. When the phrase 'Christian Church' is used it means all Christians around the world. In some churches, the lighting of a candle is a symbol of the prayers offered to God. Jesus is often referred to as 'the light of the world' so the lighting of a candle symbolises God's presence.

Pages 10/11 Most churches have a priest or minister who is responsible for leading and organising worship. In some churches it is always a man but there are male and female priests and ministers in many churches. One of the functions of the priest is to help the congregation learn and understand more about the Bible. The Christian Bible consists of the Old Testament (written in Hebrew) and the New Testament (written in Greek). Events from the life of Jesus are to be found in the New Testament in the Gospels (literally 'good news'). Both Testaments help followers to learn about the love of God for the world.

Pages 12/13 Many families have a Bible that has been passed down from one generation to another. Christians believe that the Bible can teach and guide them in daily life. One of the teachings of Jesus and the Church is that God is compassionate and will always forgive those who are truly sorry for their misdeeds. 'Sin' is the word often used for going against God's wishes.

Pages 14/15 Stained glass has been used for centuries in churches to depict events from the Bible, stories from the life of Jesus, Christian saints or significant events in a church's history. Windows can be used to tell the Christian story, as aids to worship or as a reminder of Christians who have set a fine example for others to follow.

Pages 16/17 The Christmas crib is supposed to have been first used by Saint Francis of Assisi in the 13th century. Christians did not celebrate Christmas for the first 300 years after Jesus' birth because the date was not known. It was the Emperor Constantine, in the fourth century, who decided that Christmas would be celebrated on December 25 and it has remained so ever since. Many traditions have grown up around the Christmas story which is a combination of the two different accounts which can be found in the Gospels of Matthew and Luke.

Pages 18/19 Christians exchange presents and cards at Christmas partly because the Gospel of Matthew describes wise men (magi) coming to give gifts to Jesus. It is also because, for Christians, Jesus is understood to be a gift from God to the world. In the northern hemisphere, the birth of Jesus is celebrated at a time when the days are short. Christmas lights shining in the darkness are a powerful reminder of light triumphing over darkness, goodness over evil.

Pages 20/21 Easter is the most important Christian festival. The events of the last days of Jesus' life are retold in Holy Week, the week before Easter. Good Friday, so called because of the 'goodness' of Jesus' willingness to die to save all people, is the day on which Jesus was crucified. Churches are bare and sombre but there is also a note of expectancy. Services and vigils are held as Christians share in and are reminded of Jesus' sacrifice.

Pages 22/23 On Easter Day, for Christians the day of the resurrection, there is great happiness; churches are decorated with flowers and all the colour flows back into the church on that day. Christians give thanks, for, as they believe Jesus triumphed over death, he also made it possible for them to triumph too. Christians send out cards and exchange Easter eggs. The egg is a symbol of new life about to burst forth. The empty cross, however, for Christians, is the symbol of Jesus' sacrifice for humankind and his final triumph over death.

Pages 24/25 Harvest is not officially a festival in the Christian calendar but since being 'invented' by the Vicar of Morwenstow in Cornwall in the last century, virtually every church and school has a harvest festival. Thanks are given to God for all the fruits of the earth. Gifts of food and money are given for those who are in need.

Pages 26/27 Christians want to commit their lives to each other in the presence of God. Many marriages still take place in church. The priest or minister conducts the service and the couple make vows to each other and are blessed. It is a public statement of a couple's love for each other. The party that follows, of course, is a time for families to meet, new friends are made and old acquaintances renewed.

Pages 28/29 At a baptism or christening, water is poured over the child's head and a sign of the cross made in oil on the forehead. Godparents promise to support the parents and the baby and ensure he or she is brought up as part of the Christian family. In some churches, baptism takes place when the child is older or in adult life when he or she can decide for him or herself whether to be baptised. In this case the practice is often to immerse the person totally in water.

Hello.
My name is Daniel.
I am a Christian.

Today is Sunday. It is a special day
for Christians. I have just been to
church with my family.

Why do you go to church?

We go to church to worship God together. We sing **hymns** and say **prayers**.

Why are you lighting a candle?

In our church we light candles when we pray to God.

Who is this?

Tom is our **priest**. He reads stories from the **Bible** about Jesus, the Son of God.

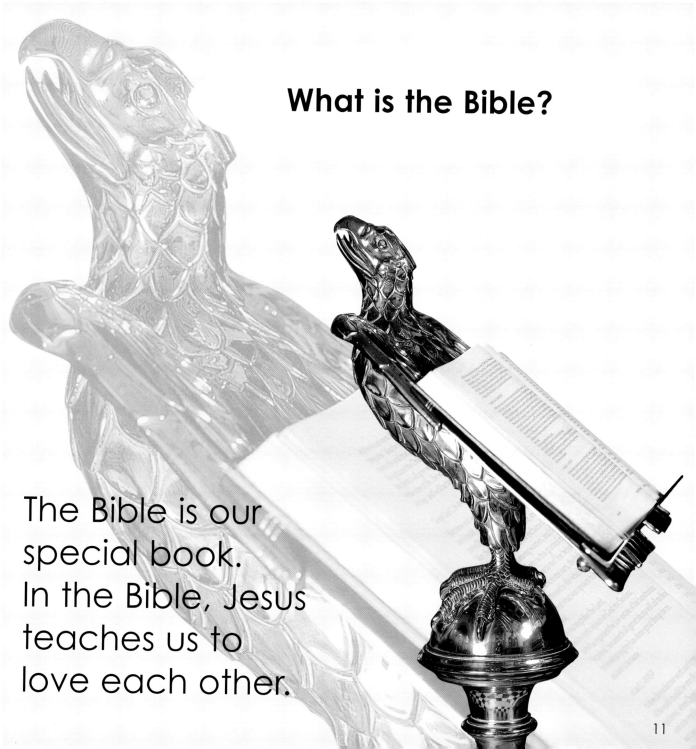

What is the Bible?

The Bible is our
special book.
In the Bible, Jesus
teaches us to
love each other.

My sister and I read stories about Jesus in our family Bible.

In the Bible, Jesus teaches us
to forgive and say sorry.
But sometimes that is hard to do!

In our church, the stained glass windows show pictures of the life of Jesus. He loved and cared for others and taught us to do the same.

What does this window show?

These are some of our **saints.** Saints are special Christians who lived good lives. We try to follow their example.

When was Jesus born?

Jesus was born 2000 years ago.
We remember his birth at **Christmas**.
Our Christmas crib has a model of
baby Jesus in the stable.

This painting
shows baby
Jesus in the
stable with his
mother Mary.

The wise men brought gifts for baby Jesus. Now, we give each other cards and presents at Christmas.

Christians believe that Jesus is the light of the world. In our church we light lots of candles at Christmas to remind us of Jesus.

Christmas is a fun time but **Easter** is happy and sad. The church looks bare and empty on Good Friday. Everyone feels gloomy.

Why is a sad day called Good Friday?

When Jesus died on the cross
he did a good thing for us.
So it is called Good Friday.

On Easter Day we are very happy because that is when Jesus rose from the dead.
Our church looks bright and new.

Why are you painting eggs?

We give each other Easter eggs to remind us that Jesus died to give us new life.

I like Harvest best. My dad is helping me to make a basket of fruit to take to church.

At Harvest we say thank you for our beautiful world and for all God's gifts to us.

Are there other special times?

Weddings are special. When Christians marry, they promise to love and care for each other. They ask God to help them when they are married.

After the wedding, there is
a big party. Everyone shares
the big wedding cake.

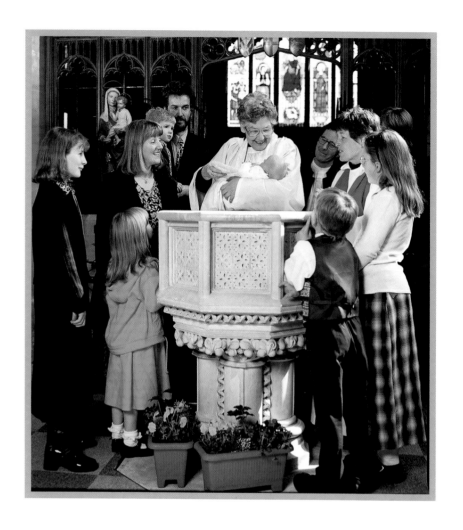

This is a special day, too.
The baby is my friend Bryony.
It is her **baptism**.

We all welcome her into God's family and promise to help bring her up in the Christian way.

Glossary

Baptism - A sign of membership of the Christian family.

Bible - The Christian holy book which is read at home and in church.

Christmas - The time when Christians celebrate the birth of Jesus.

Church - The place where Christians worship. It is also the name for people all over the world who are followers of Jesus.

Easter - The time when Christians remember Jesus died and came back to life.

Hymns - Special songs to praise God. They are often about Jesus and about living as a Christian.

Prayers - A way of talking and listening to God.

Priest - The man or woman who leads worship in church.

Saints - Special people who have shown God's love for others. Christians try to live like them.

Index